Muggins

Muggins was a very smart cow pony. He was a cross between a quarter horse and a thoroughbred. I purchased him when we moved into the mobile homes in the Silva Valley. During the early years of the development, Muggins and I covered most of the ten thousand acres in El Dorado Hills, working cattle with local ranchers and looking at new projects. When we ultimately moved from El Dorado Hills to another ranch, Muggins lived with us and several other horses until he passed away at the age of thirty years old.

THE STORY OF
EL DORADO HILLS

CARL KOWALL

WESTBOW
PRESS®
A DIVISION OF THOMAS NELSON
& ZONDERVAN

WestBow Press books may be ordered through booksellers or by contacting:

WestBow Press
A Division of Thomas Nelson & Zondervan
1663 Liberty Drive
Bloomington, IN 47403
www.westbowpress.com
1 (866) 928-1240

ISBN: 978-1-9736-0000-8 (sc)
ISBN: 978-1-9736-0001-5 (hc)
ISBN: 978-1-5127-9999-6 (e)

Library of Congress Control Number: 2017913080

Print information available on the last page.

WestBow Press rev. date: 11/13/2017

Dedicated to
Allan Lindsey—friend, ally, mentor, and boss.

"Make no little plans; they have no magic to stir men's imagination"

-Daniel Hudson Burnham

CONTENTS

ACKNOWLEDGMENTS

The following people and organizations have provided me with material or encouragement to complete this book. I am eternally grateful to each of them for their assistance and support.

Sam Abukhdair, Dr. Denny Anspach, Donald Burns, Anne Conway, Jim Cordano III, Dan Cole, Dan Corfee, Pete Thompson, Walter Dahl, Anne Dieu, Ryan Easley, Jim Lewis, Herman Lorenz, Jim Hill (Inter-County Title Co.), Lorie and Don Kowall, Moe Mohanna, Loren Lorenzen, Walter Phillipp, Bill Parker, Don Roberts, Bill Anderson (Stewart Title Company), Ernie Siller, Doug Sleeper, Jason Cheshire, Janice and Dallas Davis, Ralph and Sue Vitiello, Angela Howard, Bill Romanelli, Rosemary Neves, and Brad Murchison

THE MEMO

This is a story of the early development of El Dorado Hills. The original idea for this large development was exclusively Allan Lindsey's. Over a period of approximately ten years, he assembled and managed a very large and diverse group of people with backgrounds in the real estate industry. Allan passed away in September 2003. I am one of the few remaining people who were a part of the original team.

Several of my professional and personal friends who were aware of my experience with the project have encouraged me to write this story. I've tried hard to focus the story on El Dorado Hills and the people involved. Any references to me are purely incidental. The nature of my responsibilities as vice president of land development necessitated my involvement in almost every aspect of the project. In this story, the use of the words *I, me,* or *we* only means that I was a part of the team that got the job done.

For those of you who are not familiar with Sacramento and El Dorado County, the El Dorado Hills project is located approximately twenty-five miles east of downtown Sacramento, which is the capital of California. It's situated at the confluence of the Sacramento and American rivers. Sacramento itself is one hundred miles inland from San Francisco.

El Dorado Hills contains approximately ten thousand acres on the westernmost slopes of El Dorado County, north and south of Highway 50. At the time of our purchase, most of the land was used for cattle grazing. The elevation of the project varies from five hundred to thirteen hundred feet and is adjacent to Folsom Lake. At one point in time, the Pony Express ran through some of the land near Green Valley Road.

History tells us that during the gold rush of 1849 through the 1860s, it was commonplace for a new town to spring up wherever gold was discovered. Many of these towns became shadows of what they once were as production dropped, buildings burned down, locations were flooded out, and so on. Towns like You Bet, Indian Hill, 5-Mile House, Big Cut, and Buck Bar faded away. A few of the gold rush towns that have survived are Placerville, Grass Valley, Nevada City, Shingle Springs, Coloma, and El Dorado.

l begin this story with a copy of an internal memo my staff and I prepared during the early stages of our development activities. It provides an interesting view of the project close to the very beginning, as well as the opportunity and challenges that we foresaw.

May 5, 1960

I wish it to be clearly understood that no attempt has been made to dictate methods or the manner in which this project should be developed and sold. What we have tried to do is incorporate all the ideas and accomplishments that have come to our attention to the date of this outline. Also, we have taken the liberty to include some ideas on the various aspects of this development, which is some cases may be worthy of your opinion and, in other cases, should be disregarded. Some of the ideas and procedures submitted are results of recent experience or print articles which have been exposed to this department.

—Carl J. Kowall

El Dorado Hills: Proposed Development Outline

The proposed community of El Dorado Hills, near Sacramento, California, was conceived and planned on the "new town" principle. It can be regarded as the first new town in this area for quite some time. Although it is not in itself a municipality, it will contain a central core consisting of shopping and commercial centers, recreational attractions, office buildings, a post office, possibly a police station, a community center, etc. Around this area will be located residential neighborhoods, with anticipated industrial development located south of Highway 50, probably in the vicinity of the sewage treatment plant. It is anticipated that development will begin the latter part of this year, 1960. This project will be under the supervision of Lindsey and Company, the largest Realtor and developer in the metropolitan area. Allan H. Lindsey is the president of Lindsey and Company.

Location and Site

This development is located in the western slopes of El Dorado County and immediately east of the Sacramento County line. For a number of years, including the present, the land has been the site of cattle ranches that afford excellent spring grazing. The acquisition of approximately

10,000 acres that will make up the site of El Dorado Hills, begun in December 1958, will be completed with the exception of possibly one two-hundred-acre parcel that will be acquired shortly. In all, about twelve parcels of land were purchased, ranging from eighty acres in size to thirty-five hundred acres.

It is most likely that this land, situated in the western part of El Dorado County about twenty-five miles from the heart of the city of Sacramento and adjacent to one of the largest recreational reservoirs in northern California, namely Folsom Lake, would eventually come under some form of suburban development. The property is less than ten minutes from one of the largest industrial firms in the area, which presently employs some 25,000 people. The industrial expansion and population growth of the Sacramento area after the World War II has been somewhat phenomenal. Because of the improved highway conditions, industrial growth, and direction of this proposed development, the population trend is definitely headed in this direction.

The site of the development consists of four natural valleys, a number of scenic plateaus, and several tree-studded ridges, all of which afford excellent views of the surrounding foothills, natural valleys, the Sacramento Valley, and Folsom Lake. The soil conditions are not the most ideal, inasmuch as many areas show evidence of rock outcroppings and other areas are limited in the amount of topsoil that is available. This in itself generated problems for development, which created a necessity for unique planning with new approaches and underground and grading activities.

Advanced Planning

The planning of El Dorado Hills has been underway for quite some time. The firm of Lindsey and Company does not maintain its own planning staff. A land planner and consultant from Los Angeles [name intentionally omitted] has been retained to prepare a master plan for the total development to date. He has prepared the initial plan, including such features as major street locations, central business district, regional commercial centers, proposed recreational sites, and approximate school locations.

Lindsey and Company has contracted with the Joseph E. Spink Engineering Company to prepare all plans and specifications for this development. This engineering firm presently employs some hundred and fifty men and women and has been really responsible for a large portion of the engineering performed in this area for several decades.

The objectives of the developers of El Dorado Hills are to build an integrated community of residential, commercial, and industrial development in an area that affords a type of terrain unlike any other development in the metropolitan area, which for the most part is flat and gently rolling land. It is planned to confine the industrial development to an area south of Highway 50 and to locate the main commercial development along with community facilities along the existing Highway 50, which in the foreseeable future will be a major east-west freeway.

The residential developments will be integrated units of planned neighborhoods. The residential development will include single-family homes, duplexes, and apartment sites. It is anticipated that single-family homes will be designed to sell for approximately $15,000 up to as much as $50,000 and possibly more on lots ranging in size from seventy by one hundred and twenty feet up to one or two acres. A wide choice of apartment accommodations will be planned for corresponding ranges in rents. It is planned that within this development there will be at least one and possibly two golf courses integrated in subdivision designs.

Utilities

One of the major problems confronting the area of this development, and perhaps the paramount reason for its non-development to date, is the lack of utilities presently available to the area.

The developers have negotiated and entered into a contract with the Bureau of Reclamation for a sufficient water supply from the adjacent Folsom Lake. This water would have to be taken from the reservoir and lifted some four hundred feet, where water treatment plants will purify the water for domestic use and transport it through a series of major trunk lines and reservoirs throughout the total development.

The sewage treatment plant, along with the major trunk lines, will be constructed to allow a large portion of the development's sewage disposal to flow by natural gravity into the sewage treatment plant.

In the interest of providing the above-mentioned facilities, the developers are in the process of forming a County Water District (EHCWD) to sell general obligation bonds to finance the construction of the major water and sewage treatment plant facilities. In the agreement detailing the financing arrangement, it is anticipated that the developers will guarantee to meet the debt service on the bonds in the event the district fails to make such debt payments. It is planned that a hookup fee for both sewer and water will be charged to the builders by the water district upon the completion of their homes as constructed, and to substantially amortize and make payments on these bonds as required.

Because it is inaccessible to the existing facilities, the project will take extensive study insofar as furnishing sufficient natural gas. To this end, the developers are endeavoring to work as closely as possible with the various utilities supplying the utility services.

Schools and Zoning

Insofar as schools are concerned for this development, there are no facilities available in the immediate area. The closest elementary school is approximately 10 miles east and the the closest high school is approximately 8 miles east of the project.

It is the intention of the developers to assist the school district in every way possible to provide classroom facilities as quickly as homes are sold in the development or very shortly thereafter. To this date no direct way has been figured out on how to achieve this. It was suggested by the local school authorities that possibly some of the initial homes built in the development could easily be built in such a manner as to allow classroom facilities until such time as a demand created for an elementary school could actually be constructed with school district and state funds.

The developers have indicated that they would consider donating the first school site free; however, they did not want this to be a pattern for future school sites acquisition. So far on the approximately 7,000 acres of the development which to a certain extent have been studied to date, there will be approximately fifteen elementary school sites, three junior high schools or middle schools, and one senior high school, which total, including the adjacent parks, approximate 375 acres. This is in anticipation of El Dorado County using the case 6 school system with one junior high school for every case 6 school and one senior high school for approximately every four junior high schools.

Insofar as the zoning ordinances in this development are concerned, the areas presently zone under an emergency classification for agricultural use. It will remain so until such time as a master plan for the area has been approved and final zoning ordinances for the area have been developed. Every effort will be made between the planning officials of El Dorado County and the developers to properly zone various areas of project, in an effort to safeguard property values and sensible land uses and to further protect the development of properties beyond its boundaries in establishing future as well as present permissible land uses.

Neighborhood Planning

It is the intent of the developers to properly locate neighborhoods in such a manner as to create distinct levels of neighborhoods. Every effort will be made to blend these neighborhoods together through the use of natural conditions such as forest lines, drainage crevices, natural streams, ridgelines, and view sites.

To date, no lending institutions have been contacted for their opinions on mortgage loan conditions that will prevail when the construction of new homes begin in this project. It is anticipated that it will be possible to obtain favorable mortgages as well as full FHA approval on this development.

Such things as church sites and school sites will not be arbitrarily placed within the development but actually located and planned with each neighborhood for proper placement and usage. It is estimated that the church sites will range from 1.5 to possibly 4 acres in size.

Every attempt will be made to eliminate through traffic on all residential streets other than the major thoroughfares. To this extent, and also because of the topography, there will be considerable usage of *T* intersections and cul-de-sacs.

Whenever neighborhoods are located adjacent to major arteries, frontage roads will be employed to eliminate the necessity to back up residential lots to the main thoroughfares. This concept, however, is in conflict with the planning authorities in El Dorado County, who prefer to have residential lots back up to these major thoroughfares. It is not without foundation that the developers choose to use the frontage street method. There is visual evidence here in the metropolitan area as to the adverse effects of building backyard fences along major thoroughfares and the maintenance of them.

Every attempt will be made to achieve conformity in the construction of homes with regard to size, price, design, color, and settings, plus such things as deed restrictions relating to minimum lot widths, side-yard setbacks, fencing, garage locations, architectural control, and actual usage of land depending upon their zoning. Examples of this would be that in commercial areas, there shall be commercial use only; in multiple residential areas, only such use will be permitted; and in private residential areas, only such use shall be permitted.

Parks and Trees

Insofar as proposed parks and recreational sites in this development are concerned, it is planned to include five acres of neighborhood park sites with each elementary school location, and a twenty-acre park site adjoining the senior high school location, of which there is one. To date, there has been no solution arrived at as to how these neighborhoods and community park sites will be maintained. Some thought has been given to the possibility of forming a community services district for the maintenance of these sites, and also to perform such other functions that are not permissible under the County Water district, such as garbage collection, police protection, etc.

Existing trees located throughout this development consist of large scrub oaks, a few scattered pines, and several species of small trees. Every possible endeavor will be made to preserve existing trees in the development and subdivision design. From time to time, the developers plan to plant additional trees whenever deficiencies occur and the need arises. The manner in which this tree planning program will be conducted has not yet been worked out.

Controls

The developer will engage directly in home construction as well as land development in this project, and through its various departments will attempt to keep control over all aspects of this development wherever possible. This will include such things as enforcing permissible land uses and harmonious locations; the approval of various types of home construction, such as contemporary versus conventional; and the harmonious design and construction of such things as commercial and industrial facilities.

Building Policies

As mentioned before, the developers will also be building homes in this project. However, it is their intent also to attract as many good builders as possible to construct homes in the area. Also they will encourage each of these builders to seek the guidance of competent architects in designing their homes. Lots will be sold to these builders by various methods. Some will be fully developed lots with all improvements in, and others will be paper lots on which the builders will have to install their own improvements. It is not anticipated that acreage that has not been designed under the supervision of the developers will be sold. By doing this, they hope to able to control the total harmonious development of this project.

Architectural Design

Although developers will maintain certain control over this project, every attempt will be made for freedom of basic architectural designs. It is very probable that these controls will become valuable when lots are sold to individuals for the design and construction of their own homes.

Sales Method

Every attempt will be made by the developers to give material assistance to the various builders in this project in their efforts to sell homes, whether they are actually selling the homes for themselves or through some medium of advertisement. It is planned to have a main information office and later, if development so dictates, to have additional neighborhood tract offices that will serve as focal points for initial inquiries to potential home buyers. It is planned to devise a system whereby the various builders will contribute to the upkeep of these offices, perhaps on a per-lot basis.

A topographical model of the entire community will displayed in the information office, along with aerial photos and exhibits necessary for sales, to describe the area. In addition to this, promotional and informational literature will be available to the public.

It is being considered to set up a builders association promotional fund. The developer will match money contributed by builders dollar for dollar for project promotion. This fund will be used to promote the entire project as a whole and will be in addition to anything an individual builder will do on his own.

The developers themselves will retain the services of a public relations and advertising company to carry out this program on both a local and regional basis.

Facts and Figures

The following figures will apply to all that portion of the development that lies north of Highway 50, consisting of some 6,827 acres. This does not include another approximate 1,100 acres representing the Joerger and Burton ranches, which will be analyzed later.

Total Area: 6,827.4 acres
Land Uses:

Land exceeding 30% slope	755 acres	11.06%
Bass Lake	67.4	.99
Reservoir, Section 31	8.7	.13
Golf Course	140.0	2.06
Central Business Dist.	77.0	1.13
Motel, Medical Center, etc.	17.0	.25
3 Regional Shopping Centers	84.0	1.24
9 Neighborhood Shopping Centers	27.0	.40
High School and Park	60.0 (a)	.89
3 Jr. High Schools	90.0	1.32
15 Elementary Schools, K-6	225.0 (b)	3.30
Civic Center	10.0	.15
Hospital	13.0	.19
10 Church Sites	40.0	.59
Church Campus	15.0	.22
	1,629.1	23.89

Total Residential: 5,198.3 acres

Yield & Population		Acres	Lots (c)	FAMILIES	POP.(d)
Single Family	96%	4,990	15,968	15,968	51,098
Multifamily	4%	208	666	2,664 (e)	7459
	Totals:	5,198	16,634	18,632	58,557

Time Element

In the interest of getting the development started as quickly as possible, the developers are seeking an interim method for financing initial off-site improvements. If development were not to begin until the sale of bonds by the County Water District being formed, homes would not be ready for occupancy until approximately July 20, 1961. It is estimated that approximate seven months will be needed to construct the major off-site facilities. If the method of interim financing for off-site improvements can be worked out, homes can be constructed and ready for occupancy by approximate February 1961. The size of the initial units has not yet been determined.

Lindsey and Company

We anticipate that additional corporations and divisions will be formed. However, currently, Lindsey and Company consists of approximate thirty salespeople and twenty office people, including the following management personnel:

Allan Lindsey, president
Bob Jennings, vice president and general manager
Irvine E. Borchert, sales manager
Donald Holland, in-house legal and office manager
Leonard Brown, advertising and building supervisor
Willard Nielsen, industrial developments
Richard Hunt, commercial department
Carl Kowall, all corporate land development projects

CHAPTER

2

PROJECT FINANCING

The investment capital to finance the acquisition and development of the fifteen thousand acres we purchased was arranged by Prentice Hale and his staff. The sources of capital came from Hale Brothers Associates and their related corporations, Aqua Chemical, Union Oil Company, Bank of America, and a few private investors brought in by Prentice Hale.

The five thousand acres purchased in the Sacramento Valley were smaller parcels varying in size from five to two hundred acres. Approximately thirty-five parcels were obtained.

The El Dorado Hills land was put together by combining twelve contiguous ranches ranging in size from eighty acres to thirty-five hundred acres.

Our average cost of land in the Sacramento Valley, where the land was mostly flat, was $1,200 to $1,500 an acre. Our average cost of land in the El Dorado Hills was approximately $650 an acre.

Typical purchase agreements were cash for smaller parcels and, for the larger parcels, a 29 percent down payment with the balance in the form of a promissory note secured by a first deed of trust, usually amortized over a period of ten to fifteen years with interim and release clauses.

Wherever possible in the Sacramento valley projects, engineering and street work was financed through the use of 1911 bonds in the county, and 1913 improvement bonds when the new developments were in the city.

In El Dorado Hills, the original water take-out facilities, water treatment plant, major trunk lines, initial storage, initial sewage plant, and lift stations were all financed by the sale of 2.5 million dollars of general obligation improvement bonds. If memory serves, the initial sale to the public on these bonds was discounted around 12 percent and had a yield over the twenty-five-year life of the bond of about 5.5

percent, tax free. To my knowledge, all of the initial water district bonds have now been retired.

There are many other items and improvements that had to be covered on a cash basis, which I will describe in a later chapter.

CHAPTER 3

THE COMPANIES

Allan Lindsey joined the Moss & Moss sales staff in 1956 or thereabouts. From the outset, he worked on land sales and new subdivisions.

One of Allan's closest investors was Bill Ahern, the local manager of the Hale Brothers department store. Bill introduced Allan to his boss in San Francisco, who was the majority owner of a number of large department stores in California, plus other firms. His name was Prentice Hale. Prentice had just been named the chairman of the 1960 Winter Olympics at Squaw Valley.

This introduction led to the formation of a limited liability corporation called Retirement Activity Group

(RAG). The group objective was to purchase a large amount of land in the metropolitan Sacramento area and western El Dorado County. We intended to develop the land over a period of time as market conditions allowed, selling finished lots, paper lots, commercial sites, church sites, golf courses, and so on. RAG would be the source of capital required to purchase the land.

The first thing the group did was purchase Moss & Moss and change the company's name to Lindsey and Company. This real estate firm continued to sell residential, industrial, and retail properties including newly developed lots. At the time, they had approximately forty employees.

Another firm, Sierra Pacific Properties, was created to oversee all the development of the land projects, including entitlements, acquisition, engineering, planning, and construction. Eventually we employed a couple engineers, draftsmen, writers, and secretaries for this corporation which was ultimately managed by me.

RAG took title to all the land. The president of RAG was its only employee, and worked primarily as the secretary for Bradford, Cross, Dahl & Hefner. This arrangement was designed to help us keep our collective purchasing quiet and thus help us slow down property price inflation.

We also invested in an insurance company and a local title company for a variety of uses.

El Dorado Hills Project Corporation was formed at a later date, when we actually began developing the project.

CHAPTER 4

SIGNS OF THE TIMES

As you try to imagine what America was like when the El Dorado Hills project got underway, consider these facts:

- The NBA-championship Boston Celtics were led by Bill Russell.
- Elvis Presley was back from the army and at the top of the charts, along with Bobby Darin, Jerry Lee Lewis, and Frankie Allen.
- Folsom Dam was completed just in time to avoid a disastrous flood that would have occurred due to very heavy rains that year.
- The value of gold in 1960 was $37 per ounce.
- The war in Vietnam began in 1960.

- The first debate for a presidential election was televised between Sen. John Kennedy and Richard Nixon.
- Roger Marris hit sixty-one home runs.
- Barbie dolls were first introduced by Mattel.
- The US population was 177,830,000.
- Unemployment was at 3,852,000 workers.
- The national debt was $286.3 billion.
- The average annual salary for teachers was $5,174.
- The minimum wage was a dollar an hour.
- The "war babies"—all 850,000 of them—were heading to college.
- The new Summer Olympic Games were held in Russia. Wilma Rudolph won three gold medals in track and Mohammed Ali won the gold medal in light heavyweight boxing.
- Prentice Hale, CEO of Hale Brothers Associates, was appointed chairman of the 1960 Winter Olympics.
- The 1960 Winter Olympic Games were held at Squaw Valley, California.

Oh, and just a little bit later, in February 1962, Lorie and Carl Kowall were married in Carson City, Nevada, on Saturday and were back to work on Monday.

At this point, Allan Lindsey and his financial partners hired a national accounting firm, Larry Smith and Company, to prepare an economic analysis of the financial potential for the El Dorado Hills project. The Larry Smith report also included projected activities on the five thousand acres our corporation had purchased in Sacramento County.

These studies took approximately six months to prepare and assumed no defense spending cutbacks, normal immigration growth, and continuation of existing trends in the medical industry and the state government. The results suggested that the demand for increased housing in the metropolitan area would continue to be favorable.

Also at that time, the Aerojet Corporation in Rancho Cordova, with approximately 25,000 employees, was only ten minutes by freeway from the main gate to the El Dorado Hills project.

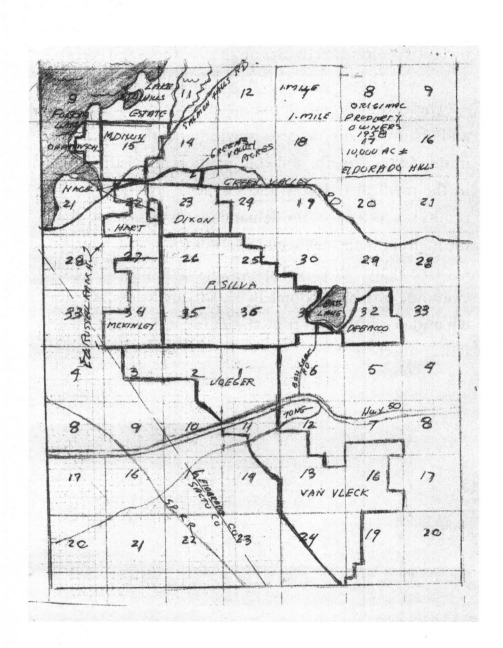

5

LAND ACQUISITION PROGRAM

At the beginning of our purchasing activities, Allan Lindsey personally worked with a broker from South Sacramento County, who indicated he could put together approximately one hundred thousand acres spread over portions of Amador, Sacramento, San Joaquin, and El Dorado counties. We realized that this land would be under several different jurisdictions, which in turn would make it more difficult to develop. So we decided to pursue a smaller program.

The acquisition of these properties was conducted by Allan and some other staff agents, including me. We decided to pursue approximately fifteen thousand acres of land, of which five thousand would be in Sacramento County and the other ten thousand, hopefully all contiguous, would be in El Dorado County. Combined, this acreage would be the basis for the El Dorado Hills project.

Most of the land in Sacramento County lay within the path of current developments. Thus, shortly after we started acquiring this land, we were able to begin work on planning entitlements, engineering, and other early stage development activities. Within a year, we brought some of the land to market as finished lots that we could build out ourselves or sell to other builders.

Other sales were in the form of so-called paper lots, which we sold to a firm called Larchmont Village. Larchmont Village was managed by Wendell and Carol Brock, who at that time ran a very successful building firm from Los Angeles. They had already built several homes in the Mather Citrus Heights area.

In the early 1960s, a paper lot consisted of a totally engineered plan with entitlements, improvement plans, and a final map ready to record. This enabled the buyer, broker, or builder to record a final map and begin construction the day after the transaction was completed. The final map was filled with the division of the real estate. In many instances today, a paper lot can be not much more than an approved study plan or tentative map.

These early developed properties, for the most part, were still untitled. So we needed to go through the process of putting the properties into drainage, sewage, water, and school districts, as well as obtain the necessary planning and engineering approvals from the Sacramento City or Sacramento County planning commissions, city councils, and boards of supervisors.

For the most part, we were able to get a yield of approximately four lots per acre, not including property set aside for commercial use, school sites, church sites and sometimes green belts and other public rights of way required by the planning commissions.

If memory serves, our average cost of a fully developed lot, including land, was about $2,700. At that time, for loan purposes, the Federal Housing Administration (FHA) would typically value these lots at $3,500 to $4,000.

In the course of developing a large portion of the Sacramento County acres, we were also able to obtain necessary entitlements and complete site preparation on three major shopping center sites: one at Florin Road and Stockton Boulevard, another at Sunrise, and Greenback Lane, and a third one at Fair Oaks Boulevard and Madison Avenue. We also prepared and sold about fifteen school sites, elementary and high school, ranging in size from ten to fifty acres.

In some instances these school sites were located where we were also developing custom lots for sale to individuals and builders. In Northridge Oaks, Fair Oaks, and South Land Park, these lots were usually larger and more expensive. The street work typically was financed with either 1911 or 1913 improvement bonds. The lot grading, the preliminary street grading, and a portion of the engineering costs were paid for in cash.

While the land cost was lower in El Dorado County, development costs were almost three times as high. In large measure this was because our yield per acre per lot was smaller, and the soil conditions made underground sewer, water, drainage, telephone, and electric services much more expensive. One of our planning goals was to put as many power and electric lines as possible underground.

While the purchase of land in the Sacramento Valley was proceeding, we continued purchasing land for the El Dorado Hills project. We purchased twelve parcels of contiguous land in El Dorado County, ranging in size from five acres to thirty-five hundred acres. Our average cost was $650 per acre. This amount, when added to our development cost, made the initial cost of a finished lot in El Dorado Hills approximately $6,000.

In all of our land acquisition programs, some of the properties were purchased for cash. But the preponderance were acquired via a purchase agreement on a typical formula of 29 percent down, with the balance payable over a period of ten to fifteen years at a market rate of interest. The promissory note was secured by a deed of trust that provided for partial release clauses as we developed the land. These partial releases also allowed us to apply the cost thereof to our annual installment payments on the promissory notes.

Most of the El Dorado Hills land was owned by local small and medium-size ranchers, as well as one or two outside owners. Almost all the land was used for raising cattle. There were only some fifteen adults living on the ten thousand acres we acquired. Some of the names were Silva, Van Fleck, Dixon, Nagel, Wolverton, Joeger, and Dong.

One of the larger parcels, approximately four hundred acres, we purchased from the Joeger family. Joe Joerger's nephew, Cal McKinley, was running the Joeger ranch, including a summer ranch of approximately one thousand acres in the Martis Valley south of Truckee. Cattle ranchers like the Joegers and Dan Russell drove their cattle over the distance to the Sierra ranches every spring and fall.

Joe Joeger had actually homesteaded the land in the late 1800s and early 1900s. Joe passed away in 1962. I will never forget his funeral in the town of Folsom. Two of his elderly friends sang "Home on the Range" and "Don't Bury Me on the Lone Prairie." At the same time, we were moving dirt on his former property a few miles up the road. It was like the beginning and the end of an era.

WATER CONTRACT

During and immediately after the purchase of the land in El Dorado Hills, we set about the task of obtaining a sustainable supply of water for the project. Without it, there simply would not be an El Dorado Hills project. There was only enough well water to satisfy the needs of a few residents and a couple thousand head of cattle. It was not nearly enough for a new community.

After our master plan was well in hand, our consultants arrived at a number of 60,000 acre-feet per year of water, which they believed would be enough to support the community when the El Dorado Hills project was fully developed.

Loren Dahl and I began the negotiations with the Bureau of Reclamation to secure the takeout of water from Folsom Lake to supply El Dorado Hills. After several months of negotiations and a few trips to Washington, I signed a contract that provided an ultimate supply of 60,000 acre-feet of water per year. The contract I signed is publicly available from the El Dorado Irrigation District.

The contract specified a minimum amount to be taken each year on a graduated, increasing schedule that had to be paid for regardless of whether the project used that much water or not. The price was nine dollars an acre-foot.

If we did not take out the designated minimum amount each year, the final allocation of 60,000 acre-feet would be reduced accordingly, so it was incumbent upon us to make sure that we met the minimum. We were able to live within that schedule for the next eight years.

In the course of obtaining this contract, we learned that it would be the last allocation of water contracted out of Folsom Lake for downstream domestic and agricultural consumption.

We also learned about the proposed Auburn Dam, which if built would hold 2.5 million acre-feet of water. Of that amount, only 750,000 acre-feet would be available for downstream domestic and agriculture use. The rest of the water would be reserved for flood control and protection.

In the event the dam was built, the allocation for domestic and agriculture use was already oversubscribed.

During the negotiations for the water contract, we decided to form a public entity to sign the contract and deliver and service the water, sewage, and fire protection facilities for the district. This entity was called the El Dorado Hills County Water District, and I was made president of the board.

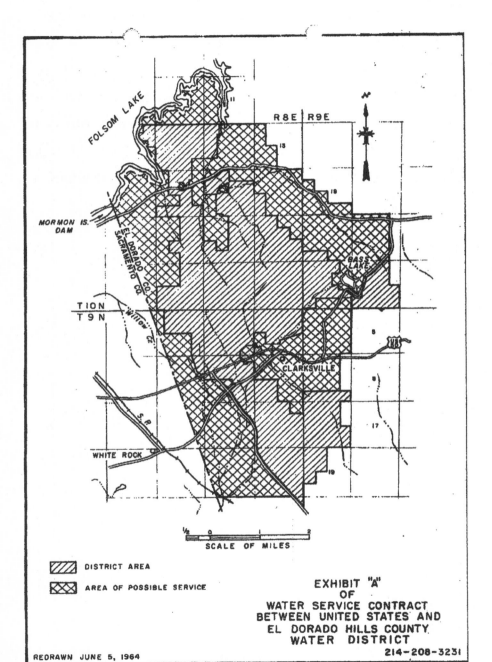

FOLSOM LAKE

R8E R9E

MORMON IS.
DAM

EL DORADO CO.
SACRAMENTO CO.

BASS
LAKE

T10N
T9N

Willow Cr.

CLARKSVILLE

S.R.

WHITE ROCK

SCALE OF MILES

⟋⟋⟋⟋ DISTRICT AREA

⧆⧆⧆⧆ AREA OF POSSIBLE SERVICE

EXHIBIT "A"
OF
WATER SERVICE CONTRACT
BETWEEN UNITED STATES AND
EL DORADO HILLS COUNTY
WATER DISTRICT

214-208-3231

REDRAWN JUNE 5, 1964

UNITED STATES
DEPARTMENT OF THE INTERIOR
BUREAU OF RECLAMATION
Central Valley Project, California

CONTRACT BETWEEN THE UNITED STATES AND RETIREMENT
ACTIVITIES GROUP PROVIDING FOR WATER SERVICE

THIS CONTRACT, made this 27 day of January, 1960,
pursuant to the Act of Congress approved June 17, 1902 (32 Stat. 388),
and acts amendatory thereof or supplementary thereto, all of which
acts are commonly known and referred to as the Federal reclamation
laws, and particularly pursuant to the Act of Congress approved August 26,
1937 (50 Stat. 844, 850), entitled "An act authorizing the construction,
repair, and preservation of certain public works on rivers and harbors
and for other purposes", as amended, between THE UNITED STATES OF
AMERICA, hereinafter referred to as the United States, represented by
the officer executing this contract, his duly appointed successor,
or his duly authorized representative, hereinafter referred to as the
Contracting Officer, and RETIREMENT ACTIVITIES GROUP, a California corporation,
with its principal place of business in Sacramento, California, hereinafter
referred to as the Contractor,

WITNESSETH, That:

EXPLANATORY RECITALS

WHEREAS, the United States is constructing and operating the
Central Valley Project, California, for the furnishing of water
for irrigation, municipal, domestic, and other beneficial uses; and

1 of 22 Pages (not included

1   IN WITNESS WHEREOF, the parties hereto have hereunto affixed

2   their names the day and year first hereinabove written.

3

4   Approved as to Legal   THE UNITED STATES OF AMERICA
    Form and Sufficiency

5

6   Attorney   By _____
    Department of Interior   Regional Director, Region 2
                            Bureau of Reclamation

7

8

9   EL DORADO HILLS COUNTY WATER DISTRICT

10   (SEAL)   By _____
                            President

11   ATTEST:

12

13   Secretary

14

15

16

17

18

19

20

21

22

EL DORADO HILLS COUNTY WATER DISTRICT

We soon learned that part of the land we had just purchased was within the boundaries of the South Side County Water District. This was an entity formed several years before to protect cattle country land from other public water allocations. Any requests for such were subject to the current property owners' approval.

Loren Dahl worked to get our recently purchased land removed from the South Side County Water District, whose mailing address was in the town of El Dorado. It took a little time and explanation about how our district would not affect their land. Ultimately, we received approval to have our land removed from South Side County Water District.

We developed a small trailer park in the Silva Valley by pouring a large slab of concrete, drilling a deep well, and installing a large septic tank system. Then we placed four mobile homes on site, brought power and telephone in, and moved myself and three of our employees with their spouses into these mobile homes. In this way, they established residence in El Dorado County and had a vote in creating the new water district. These votes were significant because, as I mentioned before, only fifteen other adults lived in the district we'd created through our land purchases.

El Dorado County began to realize that we were going to pursue approval of our project one way or another. After several hearings before the board of supervisors, we secured permission to hold an election and form a water district that followed the same boundaries as the proposed El Dorado Hills project. The election went our way, and the El Dorado County Water District was formed.

Once the election was finalized, the sale of two and one half million dollars in improvement bonds was authorized. An additional twenty five million dollars in general obligation bonds was authorized for future growth and improvements as needed. The additional bonds were approved so that we would not have to go back to the district for approval of the bonds at a later date. We were then ready to sign our contract with the Bureau of Reclamation for the water out of Folsom Lake. Simply put, this was the most significant achievement in our efforts to develop the El Dorado Hills project to date.

CHAPTER
8

MASTER PLAN

By the end of 1960, we began to create a master plan for the El Dorado Hills project. Initially we hired a local planner. After three months, he presented us with a plan that was not very imaginative, leaving everyone quite disappointed.

We continued our search for a qualified planner and subsequently hired Victor Gruen and Associates from Southern California, who came highly recommended. We outlined the goals we wanted to achieve, and they responded accordingly.

VG and Associates assigned one principal and two architects to the project. Several trips to the project site were required, and several meetings in Los Angeles and

Sacramento. It took a little less than six months to design a plan that everyone was really pleased with.

The master plan called for a series of villages, each with a few hundred lots. The villages had different themes in their names. For example, Park Village streets were named after national parks, Governors Village streets were named after California governors, St. Andrews streets were named after popular golf courses, and Crown Village streets were named after worldwide royalty.

Park Village was our first production subdivision. The lots were built out by a variety of builders, including ourselves. Crown Village and St. Andrew Village were likewise production lots. Governors Village was a "custom lot sale" and designed accordingly.

We set aside certain areas in the master plan for elementary and high schools, parks, an archery range, green belts, central shopping, industry, a garbage dump, and sewer and water plants. We also considered building a small airport runway south of Highway 50 but subsequently abandoned the idea because of a conflict with the aircraft approach to Mather Air Force Base.

The major throughway through the project was El Dorado Hills Boulevard, with a very clever body of streets for ingress and egress to the different villages. Taking into account Highway 50, we set aside enough area for an initial interchange as well as the interchange that exists today. From the beginning, we knew that efficient traffic control and convenience were required to create a quality place to live and work.

The master plan was quite comprehensive, showing land slopes, grading, soil conditions, and various requirements for tree cover.

We brought our master plan to the El Dorado County Planning Commission and the board of supervisors. For the most part, they opposed our plan. The opposition appeared somewhat arbitrary to us, since very few suggestions for changes were made. After several public hearings, Loren Dahl and Allan Lindsey, with a little help from our staff, did a masterful job in getting our plan approved.

We were now in a position to begin developing the villages. We doubted the local authorities had ever seen something of this size. Time has proved that our master plan was sufficiently prescient to accommodate the future growth and success of the El Dorado Hills project. The original design was flexible enough that new developers and builders could carry on the concept in later years.

Allan Lindsey, Lawton Langdon, and I toured several new town projects in Southern California, the eastern United States, and Canada. What we were searching for were new ideas for our project. We wanted to benefit from mistakes that similar projects had made and not duplicate them.

On tail end of the last of our project trips, Allan and I travelled back to California from Chicago, while Lawton Langdon went on to New York. Unfortunately, while there he took ill and passed away. This was a real blow for us. Lawton had been a very good friend to Allan and Prentice and was a good go-between. He was also a very intelligent and wonderful person to know and work with.

The following is a brief summary of his background:

Lawton Langdon was a 47-year old executive, son of the late State Supreme Court Justice William Langdon.

Lawton attended the University of California, Stanford and Harvard and was admitted to the Bar in 1936.

He was secretary and a director of the Hale Brothers Store, Inc. from 1946 to 1950 when he became secretary of Broadway-Hale.

He was named a director in 1956 and vice president in May of the same year. He was also executive vice president and a director of Hale Bros. Associates, Inc.

Lawton was a director of the British-American Chamber of Commerce and Trade Center and of the San Francisco branch of the American Cancer Society.

He was a member of the State Bar Association, the American Society of Corporate Secretaries, the Bohemian

Club, Commonwealth Club, San Francisco Golf Club and the Burlingame Country Club.

In spite of the difference in our age, education, and business experience, Lawton was very patient and helpful towards me.

9

EARLY DEVELOPMENTS IN EL DORADO HILLS

After we got approval from the El Dorado Board of Supervisors and Planning Commission of our master plan, we started construction on the water plant, the sewer plant, and their associated trunk lines. We soon learned that we would have to deal with the California State Parks and Recreation Department to locate and construct a water takeout facility.

Our engineers gave us plans for a few different facilities, but the department wanted an almost totally hidden one. We finally settled on two huge submersible pumps attached to a sled structure with flexible trunk lines. The lines slipped into the lake approximately one hundred feet below the high-water mark. The water was then pumped up over three hundred feet, next to a subdivision called Lake Hills Estate. From there we pumped the water through a trunk line to the new water treatment plant site, a mile north of Green Valley Road.

We were told that the quality of Folsom Lake water was around 95 percent clear, so the amount of treatment necessary would be minimal. We treated through chlorination, biofilters, and settling ponds. Treated water was pumped through another trunk line to our first million-gallon reservoir located three miles south on the ridge of Governors Village, at an elevation of approximately nine hundred feet. From this reservoir, we could serve water through gravity flow to a large portion of Park Village, Governors Village, St. Andrews Village, Crown Village, and Green Valley Acres.

Because of all the pumping and changes of elevation, we had several system problems. There was too much pressure at certain points, so we had to install pressure release stations along the major trunk lines.

The sewage treatment plant and associated trunk line presented another set of problems. The first problem came about because one half of the El Dorado Hills land sloped northward toward Folsom Lake and Sacramento County. The rest of the project, from Governors Village and below

Highway 50, sloped south toward the sewer plant on Latrobe Road.

We did not want two sewage plants in different counties to maintain and operate, nor did we want more than one government to deal with. So we decided to build a major sewage lift station near Green Valley Road. From there, we collected raw sewage from the north area and pumped it through another trunk line to a point halfway south between Governer's Village and Park Village. There, the sewage would gravity-flow through major trunk lines to the new sewage plant.

Our second problem was getting approval from the State Water Pollution Control Board to release effluent from the treatment plant into Carson Creek. It took nine months of meetings and many redesigns of the plant before we finally got approval. I believe the original capacity of the water and sewage plants were sufficient to serve approximately 2,500 homes.

After the major trunk lines for sewer and water were completed, we finished developing El Dorado Hills Boulevard and the interchange to Highway 50, which has become the major thoroughfare through the project.

Several of the original villages' engineering was being worked on while we were resolving the entitlement and design problems for our water and sewer systems. As soon as we got approval, we were able to start construction of the treatment plants and the villages simultaneously.

The first village unit we developed was Park Village, followed by Governors Village, Crown Village, St. Andrews Village, and Green Valley Acres. Our engineers and grading underground contractors had an enormous task figuring out the most economical way to move dirt and rock and dig trenches. Unfortunately, there was very little topsoil in all of El Dorado Hills, so we constantly ran into shale and other rock at every location. Some of our contractors had to use shaped dynamite charges. One contractor purchased a railroad engine and attached a huge retrenching wheel to it so as to provide the necessary force to dig a trench. As time went on and we became more experienced in subdividing the villages, we found ourselves doing less grading in preparing the lots and new street work.

To cover some early community basic needs, we called upon Union Oil Company to find a dealer for the first gas station, at the intersection of Highway 50 and El Dorado Hills Boulevard. We donated the land and did not charge the dealer any rent per month for a long period of time, until his sales volume enabled him to pay a reasonable rent. There was no specific time designated, so there was no pressure on him other than to provide good service to customers.

We also built a small market in Park Village, approximately twelve thousand square feet, and selected a small firm called Tom Thumb Market to open up a grocery store. In this case we also dedicated the land, constructed the building, and didn't charge any rent until the market showed a profit. A few other retailers were similarly subsidized as the needs of the residents demanded.

These actions laid a foundation for a full community of retail facilities, such as dry cleaners, barber shops, grocery stores, and a post office. We dedicated and frequently built facilities along El Dorado Hills Boulevard, which was becoming a very popular thoroughfare.

We were very conscious of responding to the basic needs of our early homeowners. Ultimately we formed a community services district to provide the many services that we could not provide with the water and sewer district. As it turned out, the El Dorado Hills Community Service District today is an integral part of the community and provides a lot of services for the convenience and enjoyment of the residents.

We built the first firehouse and dedicated it to the El Dorado Hills County Water District. Shortly thereafter we built the first golf course. We arranged for garbage collection. We gradually developed several small park areas. Eventually our successors also developed a park in the Silva

Valley that was named after Allan Lindsey. We continued to add retail facilities as the need arose and time and money were available. We dedicated another elementary school site in the vicinity of St. Andrews Village. There was also an additional park site created in St. Andrews Village. El Dorado Hills Boulevard was extended to Green Valley Road.

A personal friend of mine named Joe Angelo, who was an architect, designed a home for my wife and I on a couple of adjacent lots in Green Valley Acres. The design was built for us by our corporate builders. We were able to move into the new home about a year after we started construction on the El Dorado Hills project.

Once our master plan was approved, we had fewer problems processing new village subdivisions through the El Dorado County Planning Commission and Board of Supervisors.

As new developments were built, we enlisted the police department of El Dorado County to provide us with a couple officers who were dedicated to the El Dorado Hills community. One of the deputies lived in an El Dorado Hills neighborhood.

In the beginning, we recruited custom production homebuilders alongside our own building company to construct production homes in Park Village. We subsidized model home lots and production lots to outside builders until they were sold, at which time we were paid for the lots. From time to time we had promotional events to attract people to the community.

After a year and a half, the three employees and I who lived in the mobile park in the Silva Valley were able to move on to permanent homes. The other three returned to homes in Sacramento, and my wife and I moved into our newly constructed home in Green Valley Acres.

During this period, I spent about half my time in El Dorado Hills and the other half in our offices at Sierra Pacific Properties in the Lindale area. I had a staff of engineers and secretaries, two of whom were working on our valley projects and two working on the El Dorado Hills project. Until the Highway 50 freeway was fully completed, I had to pass through twenty-three red lights en route from El Dorado Hills to the office in Lindale.

EL DORADO HILLS COMMUNITY SERVICES DISTRICT

When we formed the El Dorado Hills County Water District, we knew that one day soon we would also need to form a community services district, or CSD. There were several distinctions between these entities. One was the dollar amount of general obligation bonds that could be sold for district improvements.

A CSD can provide water, sewer, and fire protection services and a host of other community services, such as parks and recreation, schools, libraries, garbage collection, public playgrounds, and so one. In that sense, a CSD is just like a charter city. However the amount of debt that a CSD can incur is limited to 15 percent of the assessed value of all the improvements and land within the district.

A county water district has no such limitation. When the El Dorado Hills County Water District was first formed in 1960, it was authorized by election to sell up to $25 million general obligation bonds. The initial sale was $2.5 million. Those proceeds were used to build the sewer plant, water plant, and trunk lines, and to buy some fire protection vehicles. The reason for obtaining $25 million in authorization was to enable the district and/or its successor to sell more general obligation bonds whenever necessary without having to seek another district vote for permission.

Another distinction we learned was that the boundaries of the CSD would have to differ from those of the water district, or the CSD would absorb the water district. This is why we purposely made the district boundaries slightly different.

When and if the citizens of the El Dorado Hills community decide that they wish to become a charter city, I'm reasonably sure that the CSD will play a major part in making that conversion possible.

When the CSD was originally formed, we hired a Sacramento attorney named Dan Gallery, who shortly thereafter became the secretary for the CSD. We had no problem finding several residents to serve on the board of directors, including my wife, who served for two years.

Early Land Development

Sunset Home Under Construction

From this model, these men will build a city for 75,000 Californians

1. **Allan H. Lindsey.** Founder, El Dorado Hills.

2. **Morgan Evans.** Horticulturist and leading conservationist. Responsible for preservation of the green belts of El Dorado Hills.

3. **Edgardo Contini, MASCE.** Chief engineer and partner. Victor Gruen Associates. Partner in charge of El Dorado Hills.

4. **Ben H. Southland.** Victor Gruen Associates. Partner in charge of planning.

5. **Larry Smith.** Larry Smith Economic Development Co.

6. **Jerome F. Lipp.** Executive Vice President and Project Manager of El Dorado Hills. President, Lindsey & Co.

7. **Dee R. Eberhart.** Western Division Manager, Larry Smith and Co. Supervisor of long term economic growth and development projections for El Dorado Hills.

8. **Douglas Baylis.** Project Landscape Architect, El Dorado Hills.

9. **Robert Trent Jones.** Robert Trent Jones, Inc. Leading golf course designer who will create the two golf courses at El Dorado Hills.

10. **Victor Gruen, FAIA.** Senior partner, Victor Gruen Associates. Internationally known architectural and engineering organization responsible for the master plan and implementation program for El Dorado Hills.

11. **Willard E. Nielsen.** Vice President, Lindsey & Co.

12. **Irv Borchert.** Sales Manager, Lindsey & Co.

13. **Robert Anshen, FAIA.** And

14. **William Stephen Allen, AIA.** Partners of Anshen and Allen. Award-winning architectural firm commissioned to design Park Village, the first unit of El Dorado Hills.

15. **William M. Anderson, Jr.** General Manager, El Dorado Hills county water district.

16. **Enoch Stewart.** Partner, Spink Engineering Company. Engineering consultant for El Dorado Hills.

17. **Brad Stark.** Assistant Project Manager, El Dorado Hills.

18. **H. D. Thoreau.** President, El Dorado Hills.

19. **Carl Kowall.** Manager, Land Development Dept., Lindsey & Co.

20. **Frank Hotchkiss.** Victor Gruen Associates. Project Manager for El Dorado Hills.

THE SUNSET HOME

During the early stages of the El Dorado Hills project, we used a host of different promotional programs to reach what we believed was a growing market for suburban living. The proximity of El Dorado Hills to Folsom Lake, the Sierra foothills, and mountain ski resorts, along with the attractiveness of the landscape, the excitement of the village concept, and the new architecture of our development all seemed to be in our favor. The new freeway also helped.

One of our challenges was to find the best ways to communicate the "new town" aspect of the project and its features to as large a market as possible. Our Bay Area financial partners had a good relationship with the Sunset

Magazine Corporation in Palo Alto, and arranged for a meeting to discuss a joint-venture promotional project.

After a few meetings, the idea emerged that the *Sunset* magazines' architectural staff would design a modern suburban home. Murchison Construction, one of our frequently used contractors, built the home on a selected lot in Governors Village. Upon completion, *Sunset Magazine* and El Dorado Hills publicized the project in such a manner as perhaps to sell more magazines and for sure to bring more people to take a look at El Dorado Hills. Within six months, the home was designed and built and a very successful promotional advertising project emerged.

In my research for this story, I was able to find four company photos from this project. Two are views of early plan development activities, and two are of the house under construction.[1]

I also found, in the Sacramento city library, an original copy of the November 1962 issue of *Sunset Magazine*, wherein twelve pages were dedicated to describing their ideas for the concept, design, and lifestyle of their "discovery home." Their ideas were intentionally controversial, in the interest of giving the reader an opportunity to view a variety of new ideas.

---

[1] I am grateful to Brad Murchison, whose family construction company built the *Sunset* home. He not only found the pictures, but provided the date when the article appeared in *Sunset Magazine*.

The article was a huge success. We did not keep track of the number of people who came to see the *Sunset* home, but the publicity certainly had the effect of increasing our sales of new residences and home sites. The promotion lasted for about six months. We subsequently sold the *Sunset* home to a family that lived there for several years and then resold the property.

The *Sunset* home is still there today. It is very attractive. It is surrounded by a host of custom homes and has become a landmark in the beautiful Governors Village.

THE FIRST GOLF COURSE

In the Victor Gruen master plan, the commercial center of town was to be located on the north side of Highway 50 and the east side of El Dorado Hills Boulevard. Approximately one hundred acres were designated for such use. In the interest of providing an attractive recreational facility we felt it would be a good idea to have a temporary use for the designated land, and so we built a golf course.

We hired Robert Trent Jones, who at the time was the country's leading golf course designer, to design a short course for us. After he completed the design, we decided to build the course ourselves. Our major grading contractor for the residential lots had some golf course grading experience, so we let him do the preliminary grading and shaping of the fairways and greens. We engaged our major underground contractor to design and install the irrigation system. We then hired an experienced golf course landscape manager to finish the tees and greens, and to manage the course after it was completed. We also constructed a small clubhouse and pro shop, and hired a young, popular professional golfer to manage the course.

On a personal note, I purchased a beautiful set of McGregor golf clubs from the pro shop at the pro's suggestion. I enjoyed them for the next thirty years. Unfortunately, when I moved back to Sacramento, someone stole the clubs and I never saw them again.

While building the golf course, we had a considerable problem due to the lack of topsoil. Many areas had to be screened of rock, and we brought in a lot of extra topsoil.

Another situation we dealt with was a number of perched water tables, or small springs. It was difficult to find where the sources were, let alone how to redirect the drainage that came from them. Our solution was that every time we ran into a perched water table, we developed another small lake. At the end of the course construction we had several such lakes, which contributed to the difficulty of play and the course's picturesque appearance.

Because the course was so popular in the early years, a lot of the initial retail development occurred south of

Highway 50—so much so that it eventually became and still is the town center.

A few years ago, the golf course was shut down due to the increased cost of maintenance and reduced usage. Some commercial establishments have been developed there. The balance was acquired by one of the later developers and is currently under consideration for other uses.

I think it is worth mentioning here that one of the later developers, Serrano, during these early years built a beautiful, full-scale, eighteen-hole golf course on top of the Silva Valley Ridge. In addition, they designed and built a wonderful clubhouse that is a credit to the golf course as well as the entire community.

CHAPTER

13

EARLY SALES AND FINANCIAL CHANGES

By 1967, we had developed more than three thousand lots outside of El Dorado Hills. Some of the lots were custom lots, but most of them were for production homes. Much of this land was in Sacramento City and some in Sacramento County. The locations were in Northridge Oaks, Barrett Hills, Barrett Meadows, Carmichael, Southland Park, and Lindale.

We obtained zoning and other entitlements for additional projects such as shopping centers, smaller retail sites, school and church sites, and so on, as I detailed in the early chapters of this book. All of these projects were very successful.

There were a few thousand acres still undeveloped, which had appreciated in value over eight years. We sold some of these parcels to other developers at a profit, and kept some of them for ourselves for future development. Our financial partners were quite pleased with our development progress and profits, and everyone was appropriately rewarded financially.

That was Sacramento County and City. The El Dorado Hills project was quite a different story.

By 1967, we had accomplished the following in El Dorado Hills:

- We had purchased approximately ten thousand acres from a dozen different owners at an average cost of $650 per acre.
- We completed a very good master plan and obtained approval from the El Dorado County Planning Commission and Board of Supervisors.
- We negotiated a contract with the Bureau of Reclamation for the last 60,000 acre-feet of water available out of Folsom Lake.
- We established a small mobile home park for four of our employees and their spouses in the Silva Valley, whereby they established residence in El Dorado County.

- We negotiated approval from the Board of Supervisors of El Dorado County to allow us to form a county water district.

- Part of that approval was the authorization to sell $25 million of general obligation bonds.

- Of that authorization, $2.5 million was immediately used to build a sewer plant, water plant, trunk lines, and takeout facilities.

- In addition, we built the pump stations and a one-million-gallon reservoir. These facilities were sufficient to serve 2,500 homes.

- Our first subdivision was Park Village, where we built our initial production homes for sale.

- We built the first fire station in Park Village.

- In Governors Village, we built two units of approximately fifty lots each.

- We completed the Green Valley Acres subdivision and sold out all of the large lots, three of which were for my first home.

- We completed El Dorado Hills Boulevard from Highway 50 to Green Valley Road, including the intersection at El Dorado Hills Boulevard and Highway 50.

- We developed a Union Oil Company service station site at the foot of El Dorado Hills Boulevard.

- We built a small grocery store and put in the Tom Thumb market.
- We built a golf course and small clubhouse at the intersection of Highway 50 and El Dorado Hills Boulevard, designed by Robert Trent Jones.
- We dedicated and helped finance construction of two elementary school sites, one in Park Village and one in St. Andrews Village.
- We developed two more subdivision units for production homes in Crown Village.
- We developed two subdivision units in St. Andrews Village for production homes.
- We began to place a number of small, convenient retail outlets south of Highway 50.
- We constructed several other miscellaneous facilities, such as an archery park.
- We planted over two thousand trees and transplanted many other types of flora throughout the project.

By the end of 1967, we had completed developing two thousand lots in El Dorado Hills.

Unfortunately, the metropolitan housing market had slowed down considerably, due in part to a reduction in workforce at the Aerojet facility. They had 25,000 employees when we began the project, but only 5,000 by the time we opened our first model home. Many of our initial buyers were employees from Aerojet, so our sales projections fell short due to the loss of this critical customer base.

Our financial partners were not comfortable with the short-range prospects for the El Dorado Hills project. They decided that they wanted not only to stop financing anything new in El Dorado Hills, but also wanted a return of some of their previous capital investments.

It took Allan Lindsey a good nine months to arrange for new financing, which we finally obtained from the John Hancock Mutual Life Insurance Company. The company provided a new loan of approximately $13.5 million. Five million was immediately turned over to our financial partners. Another five million was used to retire all the loans that were due to the original property owners. We then had $3.5 million for all the expenses that were coming due and to continue our development program for the next year.

By the end of that year, it was obvious that our sales production and cash flow were not going to be sufficient to carry the project forward without additional financing. Ultimately, we defaulted on our refinancing with the insurance company. They in turn filed notices of default and forced a foreclosure on the entire project.

In order to complete our settlement with our previous financial partners, we deeded them some of the undeveloped land that was still in our possession in the Sacramento Valley.

Allan Lindsey and our previous financial partners were the sole owners of the El Dorado Hills assets and the residual properties in the Sacramento Valley. Due to this financial setback, most of Allan's assets were heavily depleted, and so he retired to the foothills. Together with one of his brothers, he began to develop a small residential-lot sales program in El Dorado County.

I also left the project at that time and was offered a position as project manager for the Castle and Cook Corporation in Hawaii. I would have helped to develop a huge new town called Malilani, on the island of Oahu.

I had also been looking at purchasing a small industrial supply business in Sacramento. To make a long story short, I did not accept the job in Hawaii. I purchased a small firm called Sacramento Rubber Company, which was roughly eighty-five years old and had sixteen employees. It was doing a business of approximately $750,000 a year. I owned and managed the company for the next twenty years. During that time, we grew to fifty employees in two branches, doing a little over $6 million in sales a year.

At the end of the twenty years, I sold the company and came back into the real estate industry as an independent commercial broker with offices in downtown Sacramento.

For ten years, I had a very close friend named Doug Sleeper as my partner. He passed away in 2016, and I am now operating Kowall Properties on my own in downtown Sacramento. I deal mostly in income-producing properties with just a few clients, but clients that are high in quality and financial resources.

AFTER FORECLOSURE

When we defaulted on our $13.5 million loan, John Hancock immediately foreclosed on all the El Dorado Hills assets. Fortunately, the original property owners' loans had been paid off when the loan with John Hancock was established.

At this point the El Dorado Hills County Water District entered into a joint-venture agreement with the El Dorado Irrigation District and turned over to them the management and service of the water district and fire department.

The El Dorado Hills project lay idle for a few years until new developers began to purchase land from the insurance company and restart development and home sales activities. Around 1978 a developer by the name of Tony Mansour purchased the undeveloped land from the insurance company and proceeded to build and sell approximately 600 new homes. Mansour also began the development of the new town center south of Highway 50. Around 1990 the Parker Development Company purchased approximately 3500 acres from Mansour and since then have developed and sold a great many custom lots and built a beautiful golf course and clubhouse into an area referred to as "Serrano".

In retrospect, Allan Lindsey had a great idea and was truly a visionary. The biggest mistake we made was not realizing how expensive development costs would be in El Dorado Hills versus the Sacramento Valley. No one could have projected the significant drop in employment at Aerojet.

In the course of researching other projects and ideas, we learned that more often than not, the original developers of new towns go broke. The next developers that come in usually break even or make only a small profit. The third wave of development is able to benefit from all the preceding mistakes and conditions to make a good deal of money.

Today there are still a few thousand acres of undeveloped land in and adjacent to El Dorado Hills. I recently became aware of a hundred-acre sale of undeveloped land priced in excess of $100,000 an acre. What a far cry from the original $650 an acre that we paid! In the beginning of our sales programs, a typical lot in Governors Village sold for $6,000 to $10,000. A similar lot today would sell for over $150,000.

CHAPTER

15

THE HUMAN EXPERIENCE

I have spent a great deal of time on the activities and events that are part of developing a new town. In this chapter I would like to share some of my personal experiences with people who are worthy of note.

Loren Dahl was a senior partner in the law firm of Bradford, Cross, Dahl and Hefner. He was selected in the very early stages of this project to assist us in most legal matters. These included entitlements, ordinances, contracts, and so on with federal, state, county, and other public entities.

Loren was a key figure in the painfully slow negotiations for our water contract with the Bureau of Reclamation. Many more challenges followed, such as the formation of the El

Dorado Hills County Water District and the El Dorado Hills Community Service District, negotiations with the state water pollution and control board, and endless meetings with the El Dorado Hills County Planning Commission and Board of Supervisors to gain approval of our master plan. Loren's knowledge of community law and his personal relationships were crucial in moving our project forward.

After the project was well underway, Loren stayed on with us as legal secretary for the El Dorado Hills County Water District. His role was to guide us in developing the project in accordance with an enormous number of specifications and ordinances for the construction, maintenance, and operation of water and sewer facilities and the fire protection unit.

In the course of these events, Loren also became my personal attorney. Loren's tremendous relationship skills were something to admire. As a private citizen, he was very supportive of the Boy Scouts of America and was inducted into their hall of fame. Near the end of his legal practice, in 1980, he was appointed to serve as a US bankruptcy judge in the Eastern District of the State of California. My friends in the legal field tell me he served as a fair and just judge for several years with great distinction. Both of Loren's children, a son and daughter, have followed in his footsteps by forming a bankruptcy law firm of their own.

Lawton Langdon was a significant part of Hale Brothers Associates top management and was also a personal friend of Prentice Hale, the CEO. I took several trips with Lawton and Allan Lindsey to visit other projects around the country. In spite of the difference in our ages and experience, Laughton was very patient and kind to me.

Lawton's biggest role in the project was that of a go-between for Allan Lindsey and Prentice Hale. Laughton liked Allan Lindsey very much and was enthusiastic about the El Dorado Hills projects. He did all he could to help Allan in his interactions with Prentice. It was very unfortunate for everyone when Lawton passed away on our last trip to New York City. When I went to his funeral in San Francisco, it was obvious he was respected by a large group of people. Lawton was a very successful businessman and a wonderful human being.

As I've referenced before, the project team moved four employees and their spouses, including my wife and I, into a four-unit mobile home park in El Dorado Hills. I don't think my new wife was thrilled about the mobile home, having just left her parents' lovely home in Land Park. But she made the adjustment very quickly. Because we were all part of Lindsey and Company, we were all dedicated to the project. Over the next one and a half years, the group became very compatible.

There were no children in the park, but there were a couple pets. My wife and I had a beautiful German shepherd, a funny little cat, and a young cow pony called Muggings. None of us had ever lived in a mobile home before; it was quite a new experience for us all. We shared a small laundry, a newly developed deep-water well, an extra-large septic system, a couple telephone and power lines, and a large barbecue pit on the mutual patio. We also collectively endured the heavy rains and winds because there was no tree shelter.

We sort of became one family. We ate out at many of the foothill restaurants, including Poor Red's in the small town of Eldorado. We traded off going to the highway to pick up the mail, and running errands to Folsom.

We had several barbecues together. We enjoyed the sunsets and cool evenings while listening to cows mooing and coyotes howling. Several deer came and went. A very large flock of Canadian geese often fed on the grass hills surrounding the mobile homes. It was a dedicated, friendly, and successful group, very capable and unselfish.

For about a year and a half and we got along fine, living close together in the middle of a 10,000 acre cattle ranch. Our main purpose in moving into the trailers, of course, was to establish residence so we could petition and form a vote for the El Dorado Hills County Water District. We were successful in that aim. Then the company contractor completed my house in Green Valley Acres, and all of us moved out of the park.

Early in the project development, many residents were engineers, scientists, technicians, and professionals. They were a special group of adventurous people who thoroughly enjoyed the new town atmosphere. We had no trouble getting volunteers for the board of directors for the water district, the service district, fire department, and community clubs.

It seemed like everybody knew everybody. We formed a bowling league that got together every week in the town of Folsom. There were small parties and neighborhood barbecues galore. Groups were formed by many of the ladies to assist the teachers in the temporary elementary schoolrooms. Another lady put out a weekly tabloid with announcements and descriptions of events. The archery range became very popular. The needs to be served by the community service district were defined by the citizens. And it seemed everybody was hard at work on their landscaping

In the early years at Christmas time, the volunteer fireman pulled out all their vehicles and loaded them with children and adults. They drove all over the project, singing Christmas songs and throwing small gifts to children. The last stop of this event was always the driveway of my home in Green Valley Acres. My wife and I would set up a small buffet with snacks and a bar for holiday refreshments, and we sang songs and wished Merry Christmas to everybody. This went on for several years; everyone participating really looked forward to and enjoyed it.

The community had very little crime in those days. However, at one point our new home was broken into by two male thieves. They stole much of my wife's clothing and a few personal things. My wife had just pulled into the driveway with our two children in the car as the thieves were leaving. Our driveway was quite narrow, and my wife would not let them get past her. She later realized this was not the correct thing to do, but she was so mad at the time that she told them to throw everything on the ground— otherwise she was not going to move her car. Suffice it to say they obeyed, and my wife let them leave. We reported the event to the authorities, of course, but the thieves were never caught.

Not too long after that, we made a deal with the county to assign two deputies to the El Dorado Hills Project. I'm sure there are still many deputies working and living there today.

Some of the early classrooms were in a few of the newly built but unsold homes. Many parents volunteered to help the teachers and kids in the educational process. Several other people created all sorts of picnics and other events for children. It was a wonderful experience to be a part of these activities.

From the very beginning of the project, the Spink Engineering Company was involved. The land had never been accurately surveyed. A good survey was necessary if the area was to become a highly developed. In addition, there were normal new engineering requirements for the subdivision lots and underground facilities.

The Spink Engineering Company had five principal owners, including Joe Spink, Enoch Stewart, Mel Stover, Sid Steinchfield, and Don Dean, all of whom were civil engineers. They had a large staff of draftsmen, surveyors, and technicians, and at that time they were the largest engineering firm in the area. They were very capable and, fortunately, very dedicated to helping us develop a good project. We also used their firm for most of our subdivisions in the Sacramento Valley.

Grading and trenching were real challenges in El Dorado Hills. The soil conditions were quite different from the ones in the valley. In the interest of finding a better and cheaper way to move rock, one of our contractors invented what at that time was called a *shaped dynamite charge* for rock removal.

Another underground contractor, Bob Delzer, purchased a railroad engine and converted it into a trencher. It had a huge, diamond-spoked wheel with a lot of weight and power to cut through the soil and rock. It was quite a sight to see this railroad engine digging trenches. The strategy was successful, and it increased production as well achieving some reduction in cost.

Bob Albrecht was the president of Wismer and Becker. He was very helpful in developing new specifications for underground electric and telephone and securing the PUC approval for the new process.

Each week I had to split my time between El Dorado Hills and the company's Sierra Pacific properties in the valley. My staff and I met on Fridays to review activities from the previous week and outline our goals for the following week. There were so many things going on simultaneously and so much money at stake, we needed to be on top of everything we could. Our main responsibilities were to see that development activities were done right and the cost reflected the agreed-upon contract.

My wife and I loved our new home in Green Valley Acres. We had the opportunity to make friends with a lot of new people. I originally grew up in Pittsburgh, Pennsylvania, and came to California after I spent three years in the service. My wife and her parents were born and raised in Sacramento, so most of her friends were in Sacramento. Many of these friends visited us.

Our son's first school was in Rescue, California. The school bus picked him up at our driveway and got to the school after a long one-hour ride because it picked up children from all over the foothills. We were quite pleased with his early education experiences.

My personal involvement in this development project for approximately ten years had a significant impact on my life. There are a few times I would like to forget, but for the most part I was very fortunate to work with so many good and talented people, especially Allan Lindsey, Loren Dahl, and Lawton Langdon.

EL DORADO HILLS TODAY

This story would not be complete without describing the community of El Dorado Hills as it is today. It's been almost sixty years since we first moved eight people into a small mobile home park in the Silva Valley. Today El Dorado Hills is a thriving community that is being written about regularly as a wonderful place to live, work, play, and raise a family.

My wife and I have some close friends living in the project. I had the opportunity to interview some of the current residents, developers, and merchants. I learned a great deal about the current status of the project.

The current population of El Dorado Hills is estimated to be 45,000 people in 15,000 residential units.

There are several public schools physically located in Greater El Dorado Hills:

- Six elementary schools, including William Brooks, Oak Meadow, Silva Valley, Jackson, Lake Forest, and Lake View
- Two middle schools, including Rolling Hills and Marina Village
- Oak Ridge High School

In addition, there are privately operated schools such as those connected with a church congregation. Students from El Dorado Hills can also attend certain schools outside the area, including Ponderosa High School in Cameron Park and Union Mine High School in Placerville.

The educational facilities in the community are quite impressive and are conveniently located throughout the area. The school districts have distinguished themselves in the quality of education they provide.

There are a total of eight places of worship. Many denominations and faiths are represented in the project and in other nearby communities.

A few hours' drive through the El Dorado Hills project will reveal an impressive variety of architecture. There is very little flatland. Each residence has been carefully situated on its lot to take advantage of such things as slope, drainage, access, views, and foliage. The houses are well maintained and attractively landscaped. The residential streets are convenient, and one can drive throughout the project on major thoroughfares like El Dorado Hills Boulevard and Silva Valley Boulevard.

The Serrano Development Corporation publishes a quarterly magazine that features community activities and developments, along with many advertisements from local organizations and businesses, and interesting stories about individuals or corporate projects. There is quite a selection of home sites and residences available for sale. The price of finished homes ranges from $400,000 to $2,000,000.

The El Dorado Hills Community Service District has prepared a very impressive updated master plan that describes the district's administration of recreational facilities and community activities. A copy of this plan is available at the district office. The district's role in the quality of life and community activities is quite obvious. Several hundred acres of parks and other facilities are spread throughout the community. I believe that when and if the residents ever decide to make El Dorado Hills a charter city, the community service district will play a major role in such an event.

The town center is located on the south side of Highway 50 and along Latrobe Road. The town center provides a very good mix of retail, office, professional, food, and miscellaneous spaces that leave little to be desired. In addition, there are a variety of smaller commercial outlets spread among the villages.

El Dorado Hills' location makes it easy to visit many historical sites in the nearby foothills. The Sacramento County town of Folsom has evolved into quite a suburban community and is only a few minutes down Highway 50. Further up Highway 50 are some of the Sierras' most challenging ski resorts, along with all of the recreational activities associated with beautiful Lake Tahoe.

When my wife and I occasionally drove to Lake Tahoe and came home on Highway 50, I got a feeling of satisfaction as we passed Cameron Park and start down the last grade into the Silva Valley and El Dorado Hills Boulevard. It is a particularly rewarding experience in the latter part of the day, as the sun is setting and the community lights begin to come on. I remember when there was nothing but bare land here, with cattle grazing on grassy slopes.

The thing that separates this project from other communities is the spirit of the people living, working, and involving themselves in the many activities available in the community. This is the project Allan Lindsay envisioned when we began to purchase the land. I believe he would be quite pleased to see El Dorado Hills as it is today. If you have not seen the project, give it a try—I don't think you will be disappointed.

AFTERWORD

In writing this story, I have tried to keep things in perspective and make the narrative informative. Developing El Dorado Hills was nothing like going to the moon or climbing Mount Everest. It was simply a long journey.

Allan Lindsey had a dream of developing a new town, and he was able to dedicate himself to fulfilling that dream. All of us who helped him were just a part of his army. We were very proud to accomplish the beginning of El Dorado Hills together.

I cannot speak for Al Lindsay because he is no longer with us. But if you were to ask me whether, if given another opportunity to develop a new city, I would try again, the answer would be yes. However, one thing for sure would be different. We would seek a financial partner that understood the risks and rewards of real estate development and, given the size of such a project, would fully support and continue to underwrite the project in difficult as well as good times.

In my current brokerage business, I have a client who has had the same financial partner for the last thirty years. He's told me that during good times this partner is very good to work with, and during bad times they are even better. Both of these firms are quite large and very successful.

I will close by once again giving a great deal of credit to the developers, builders, merchants, and residents who continued to develop the project after our initial efforts.

That's my story of El Dorado Hills.

Carl J. Kowall

APPENDIX: ALLAN H. LINDSEY

Allan Lindsay was born on November 20, 1920, in Kahlotus, Washington. He grew up on a ranch in Corning, California. After graduating from high school, he and a friend operated a dairy for short time.

Allan then moved to Tacoma, Washington, where he worked in a shipyard as a welder with his brother Chuck. He subsequently moved to Vancouver, Washington, in May 1941, where he worked as a welder for the Kaiser Corporation and became a foreman and a welding instructor.

In 1944, Allan enlisted in the army, scoring at the top of his entrance exam class. He was assigned to go to a navigation school for cadet training. He also completed several college courses. After graduating, he became a navigator on B-17 bombers and the successor B-29s.

After leaving the military, he and his wife Ida moved to Portola, California, where he opened a jewelry store with his brother Bill. About five years later, he moved to Sacramento and took a position in an electroplating shop at Mather Air Force Base.

Shortly thereafter he made his first investment in real estate, purchasing a small parcel of land and dividing it into several lots.

Not too long after that, he was hired by the real estate firm of Moss and Moss, where he continued to sell and make land investments and subdivide properties for himself and for Moss and Moss. At that point, his development activities were in Barrett Meadows, Barrett Hills, Southland Park, Merryhill, and a couple of shopping centers.

Allan met Prentice Hale, the CEO of Hale Brothers Associates, through one of his customers named Bill Ahearn, who at the time was the manager of the Broadway Hale store in downtown Sacramento. Allan joined with Prentice Hale to form a limited partnership, the purpose of which was to acquire a large amount of land in Sacramento and El Dorado County. The plan was to develop and sell subdivisions in the Sacramento Valley, and to develop a new-town project in El Dorado County.

The story of El Dorado Hills is in large measure a product of Allan's ideas and management direction. For the next ten years, very few major decisions were made regarding Lindsey and Company, Sierra Pacific Properties, Retirement Activities Group, or the El Dorado Hills Corporation without Allan's direction and approval. In addition to providing management skills and salesmanship, he participated in as many business activities as time permitted. Most of Allan's time was spent on securing financing, working with his partners, and putting together a team of people, including me.

After the El Dorado Hills project was foreclosed upon, Allan retired to the foothills and continued to develop small subdivisions there.

Allan passed away on September 25, 2003. Before his death, he was honored by the El Dorado Hills community for his efforts in starting the project. A park was named after him in the Silva Valley.

Allan had many close friends in the industry and the community, including me. Besides being my boss, he was also my mentor and my strongest supporter.

ABOUT THE AUTHOR

60 years ago

Carl Kowall was born in Pittsburgh, Pennsylvania, in 1930. He attended Catholic grade school and a public high school, where he enjoyed athletics and lettered in swimming, track, and football.

After graduating from high school, Carl traveled to Sacramento, where he lived and worked with one of his uncles.

In the early 1950s, he returned to Pittsburgh and joined the United States Coast Guard, in which he served for three years. His military assignments included an educational program in damage control and a tour aboard a destroyer escort in the Atlantic, where he and his shipmates logged more than 300,000 miles at sea. He attained the rank of first-class petty officer.

After leaving the service, Carl married his high school girlfriend and they returned to Sacramento. His wife took a teaching job at a women's juvenile detention center while Carl attended Sacramento City Junior College on the GI Bill. The young couple then moved back to Pennsylvania, but soon separated. Carl returned to Sacramento once again.

Over the next five years, Carl worked as a junior mechanical engineer, developing production drawings for a school furniture manufacturing company while also attending Sacramento State College. In 1958 he took a position as a residential real estate salesman at the Moss and Moss real estate firm. He remained with that company and its successors for the next ten years. He also married his second wife, Lorie. The story of those ten years is the story of the origin of El Dorado Hills.

After leaving El Dorado Hills in 1968, Carl purchased a small industrial distribution firm in Sacramento. He successfully owned and managed the Sacramento Rubber Company for the next twenty years. During this period, Carl also completed a three-month MBA course called the Stanford Executive Program.

Carl went on to teach classes and serve as a guest lecturer on principles of real estate at Sacramento State College and the University of San Francisco, where his brother Richard was the director of the paralegal program. Around 1970 Carl and his wife purchased a small farm in Clarksburg, where they bred and raced quarter horses and thoroughbreds.

Today Carl still works as an independent commercial real estate broker with an office in downtown Sacramento. He and Lorie have been happily married for fifty-five years, raised two children, and are enjoying two beautiful granddaughters.

This is his first book.

Printed in the United States
By Bookmasters